Vancouver Public Library

W9-CRZ-495

Big
Science Ideas

What is a
Herbivore?

Bobbie Kalman

🌱 **Crabtree Publishing Company**

www.crabtreebooks.com

Big Science Ideas

Created by Bobbie Kalman

Dedicated by Reagan Miller
For my grandmother, Helen Miller, with love

**Author and
Editor-in-Chief**
Bobbie Kalman

Editors
Reagan Miller
Robin Johnson

Photo research
Crystal Sikkens

Design
Bobbie Kalman
Katherine Kantor
Samantha Crabtree (cover)

Production coordinator
Katherine Kantor

Illustrations
Barbara Bedell: pages 5, 14, 16 (dormouse), 29
Antoinette "Cookie" Bortolon: page 12
Katherine Kantor: pages 21, 26, 30
Jeannette McNaughton-Julich: page 24
Bonna Rouse: pages 4 (right), 16 (parrot)
Margaret Amy Salter: pages 4 (left), 11, 15, 19
Tiffany Wybouw: page 8

Photographs
© Babs & Bert Wells/OSF/Animals Animals - Earth Scenes: page 21
© BigStockPhoto.com: pages 17, 23 (bottom)
© Kathy Boast - www.kathyboast.com: page 8
© Dreamstime.com: page 25 (bottom)
© iStockphoto.com: front cover, pages 7 (bottom), 9, 27 (bottom)
© Bobbie Kalman: page 30
© ShutterStock.com: back cover, pages 1, 3, 4, 5, 7 (top), 10, 11, 12, 13, 18, 19 (left),
    20 (top), 22, 23 (top), 24, 25 (top), 27 (top), 28, 29, 31
Other images by Adobe Image Library, Corel, Creatas, and Digital Vision

Library and Archives Canada Cataloguing in Publication

Kalman, Bobbie, 1947-
    What is a herbivore? / Bobbie Kalman.

(Big science ideas)
Includes index.
ISBN 978-0-7787-3275-4 (bound)
ISBN 978-0-7787-3295-2 (pbk.)

    1. Herbivores--Juvenile literature. I. Title. II. Series.

QL756.5.K348 2007   j591.5'4   C2007-904232-5

Library of Congress Cataloging-in-Publication Data

Kalman, Bobbie.
    What is a herbivore? / Bobbie Kalman.
        p. cm. -- (Big science ideas)
    Includes index.
    ISBN-13: 978-0-7787-3275-4 (rlb)
    ISBN-10: 0-7787-3275-4 (rlb)
    ISBN-13: 978-0-7787-3295-2 (pb)
    ISBN-10: 0-7787-3295-9 (pb)
    1. Herbivores--Juvenile literature. I. Title. II. Series.

QL756.5.K43 2007
591.5'4--dc22

                                2007026960

Crabtree Publishing Company

www.crabtreebooks.com   1-800-387-7650

Copyright © **2008 CRABTREE PUBLISHING COMPANY.** All rights reserved. No part of this publication may be reproduced, stored in a retrieval system or be transmitted in any form or by any means, electronic, mechanical, photocopying, recording, or otherwise, without the prior written permission of Crabtree Publishing Company. In Canada: We acknowledge the financial support of the Government of Canada through the Book Publishing Industry Development Program (BPIDP) for our publishing activities.

**Published in Canada
Crabtree Publishing**
616 Welland Ave.
St. Catharines, Ontario
L2M 5V6

**Published in the United States
Crabtree Publishing**
PMB16A
350 Fifth Ave., Suite 3308
New York, NY 10118

**Published in the United Kingdom
Crabtree Publishing**
White Cross Mills
High Town, Lancaster
LA1 4XS

**Published in Australia
Crabtree Publishing**
386 Mt. Alexander Rd.
Ascot Vale (Melbourne)
VIC 3032

Contents

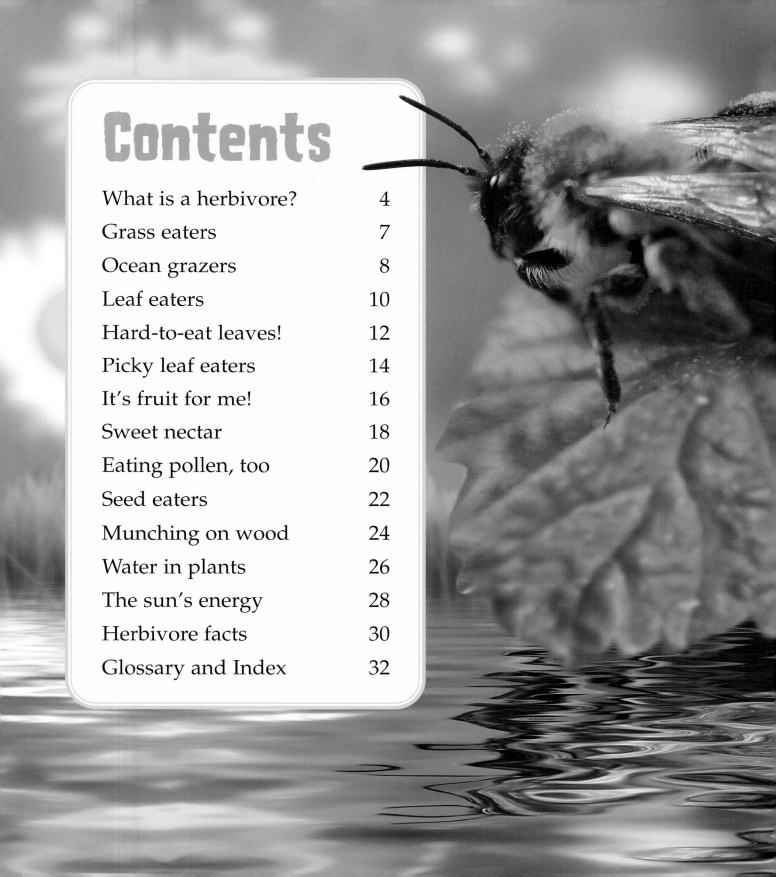

What is a herbivore?

Animals are living things.
All living things need food.
Food gives living things **energy**.
Animals need energy to grow.
They need energy to move.
They need energy to stay alive!

Hippos are big animals. This hippo is eating grass. It eats other plants, too.

Plant eaters

Animals eat different kinds of foods. The bodies of animals are suited to the kinds of foods they eat. Some animals eat mainly plants. Animals that eat mainly plants are called **herbivores**. Herbivores do not all eat the same kinds of plants. They also do not eat the same parts of plants. When they cannot find enough plants to eat, some herbivores will even eat insects or other animal foods.

Some herbivores are very small. Bees are herbivores.

Grass eaters

Many herbivores are **grazers**. Grazers eat grass and other plants that grow close to the ground. Horses are grazers. They have special stomachs that can break down the grasses they eat.

This mother horse is grazing while her baby drinks her milk. The baby will soon eat grass, too.

Rhinoceroses, elephants, and hippos are some of the biggest grazers. They eat huge amounts of grass. When there are not enough grasses to eat, these animals eat the woody parts of bushes or trees. Some grazers, such as elephants and zebras, live in big groups called **herds**.

*Elephants live and graze in herds. These elephants live in Africa on grassy places called **savannas**.*

Ocean grazers

There are grasses in oceans, too. One of the animals that feeds on sea grasses is the green sea turtle. Green sea turtles live in shallow ocean waters, where they find plenty of sea grasses to eat.

manatee

Manatees and dugongs

Dugongs and manatees are the biggest ocean grazers. They are like vacuum cleaners when they graze. They can clean an area of grasses in a short time. Both dugongs and manatees are **mammals**. Mammals breathe air above water.

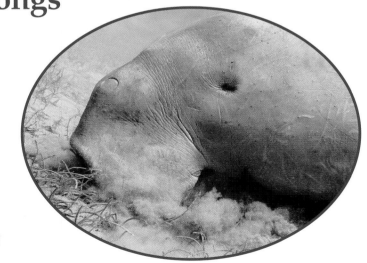

This dugong is using its powerful jaws to pull up grasses from the ocean floor.

Leaf eaters

Many herbivores **browse**, or eat leaves. Birds called hoatzins, shown here, eat mainly leaves. Hoatzins live in rain forests. The bodies of hoatzins are able to **digest**, or break down, the hard leaves of rainforest trees.

Caterpillars are insects that eat leaves. They need to eat leaves to grow. They eat a lot of leaves before they become butterflies! This monarch caterpillar eats and eats. It will no longer eat leaves once it becomes a butterfly.

Hard-to-eat leaves!

Conifers are trees with cones. The leaves of conifers are like needles. They are sharp and hard. Moose are one of the very few animals that can eat these tough leaves.

That tastes bad!

The leaves of acacia trees are also hard to eat. Giraffes can reach these leaves, but they cannot eat too many. A few minutes after a giraffe starts eating the leaves, the acacia tree makes the leaves taste bitter. Giraffes must then move to new trees to eat.

Picky leaf eaters

Koalas are picky eaters. They like to eat mainly the leaves of eucalyptus trees. Eucalyptus leaves are poisonous to other animals. Eucalyptus leaves would make other animals sick. Koalas spend most of their time in trees.

*Koalas are mammals called **marsupials**. Marsupial mothers have pouches for carrying their babies.*

Make mine bamboo!

Pandas are also picky leaf eaters. They eat mainly bamboo leaves and stems. Bamboo does not give pandas many **nutrients**, so they need to eat a lot of these plants. Pandas are **endangered animals**. There are only about 1500 pandas left in the world. Most pandas live in special parks, where they are safe from people who might harm them.

It's fruit for me!

Some herbivores eat mainly fruit. Many birds eat fruit. Dormice also eat fruit. Fruit ripens at different times, so many fruit eaters also eat other kinds of foods, such as leaves or flowers. Monkeys and apes eat fruit and other foods.

parrot

dormouse

This animal is an orangutan. Orangutans are apes. They spend most of their time in trees. Orangutans eat mainly fruit.

Fruit bats

Many bats eat insects, but some bats eat fruit. This Egyptian fruit bat is a fruit-eating herbivore. It has big eyes and a very good sense of smell.

Seed carriers

Fruit bats eat fruit or crush it to drink its juice. Most fruit bats also lick the **nectar** inside flowers. Nectar is a sweet liquid. Fruit bats carry the seeds of fruits from one place to another. They help new plants grow.

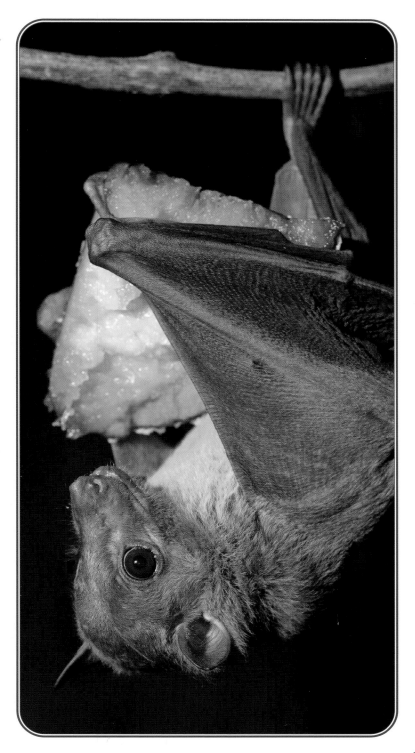

Sweet nectar

Many animals eat the nectar in flowers. Many birds feed on flower nectar. Hummingbirds are well suited to eating nectar. Their long, thin beaks can reach inside flowers to suck up the nectar. Hummingbirds flap their wings quickly to stay in place so they can eat from a flower.

Butterflies

Butterflies and moths fly from flower to flower to drink nectar. A butterfly has a mouth part called a **proboscis** that can reach inside flowers to get nectar. The proboscis curls up when the butterfly is not using it. It then opens into a long straw again to reach into flowers.

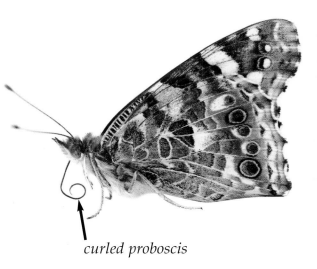

curled proboscis

Eating pollen, too

Pollen is a yellow powder found in flowers. All bees and some wasps eat pollen. Butterflies, beetles, and flies eat some pollen, too, but they mainly feed on nectar. Other pollen eaters include honey possums.

This bee is covered in pollen. It will eat both the nectar and pollen of this flower.

Honey possums do not eat honey.
They eat nectar and pollen. Their
long snouts reach the nectar inside
flowers, and their bristly tongues collect
the pollen. The honey possum is one of
the very few mammals that eats mainly
nectar and pollen. It also eats
some insects from time to time.

Seed eaters

Many insects and birds eat **grains**. Grains are the seeds of plants. Small animals such as squirrels and mice eat grains, but they eat other foods, too. Many grain eaters eat other foods.

Seed-eating birds

The birds you see at feeders eat seeds. Many seed-eating birds also eat insects, but goldfinches eat mainly seeds. This yellow bird is a goldfinch. It is eating thistle seeds at a feeder.

The crossbill has a special beak that can take out the seeds from pine cones.

23

Munching on wood

Beavers use wood to build homes called **lodges**. They also eat the twigs and woody stems of trees. Beavers have long teeth that keep growing. Their teeth are perfect for chewing wood. Beavers can even cut down big trees using their teeth!

Wood is good!

Termites eat dead wood and leaves. Some people think they are pests because they chew wood in houses and do a lot of damage. In nature, termites are very important. They help break down dead wood and other plants so new plants can grow.

*Termites build huge homes called **mounds**.*

These termites are inside their mound.

25

Water in plants

Animals cannot always find enough water to drink. Animals that live in deserts cannot find much water because deserts are very dry places. Desert animals get most of their water from the food they eat. Cactuses are desert plants that store a lot of water. When animals eat cactuses, they get water as well as food.

This iguana is getting water and food from eating a cactus plant.

Flowers and fruit

Flowers and fruit contain water, too. Deer, rabbits, and groundhogs eat flowers and fruit. These foods are perfect for young animals. They are moist, soft, and easy to chew.

Fruit contains water. This lemur is eating a watermelon.

This flower eater is a rock hyrax. It is related to elephants and horses, but it looks more like a groundhog.

The sun's energy

People and animals get energy from food, but all energy comes from the sun. Plants are the only living things that can use the energy of sunlight to make food. Plants use some of the food they make and store the rest. Herbivores eat plants. They are the first living things to use the energy of the sun that is stored inside plants. The sun's energy is then passed to other living things in a **food chain**.

A food chain

A sunflower makes food using the energy of the sun. Some of the sun's energy is in this sunflower.

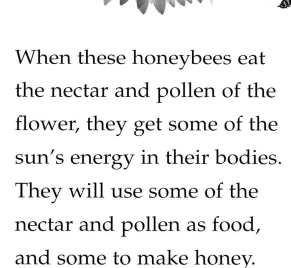

When these honeybees eat the nectar and pollen of the flower, they get some of the sun's energy in their bodies. They will use some of the nectar and pollen as food, and some to make honey.

When people eat honey, or when animals eat bees, they get the energy of the sun, the sunflower, and the bees. The sun's energy is passed along in a food chain.

honey

Herbivore facts

Most people eat both meat and plant foods, such as fruits and vegetables. People who eat only plant foods are called **vegetarians**. This girl is eating different kinds of plant foods. Name three plant foods in the picture.

Special names

Herbivores eat different kinds of foods. Some herbivores eat mainly one kind of food, such as grass. Herbivores that eat mainly one kind of food have special names. These names are inside the yellow box. On a piece of paper, write down the names. Then guess the food that each type of herbivore eats. The answers are in the pink box.

Herbivore name

1. grazer
2. folivore
3. frugivore
4. nectarivore
5. palynivore
6. granivore
7. xylophage

Answers

7. wood
6. grains
5. pollen
4. nectar
3. fruits
2. leaves
1. grasses

What do they eat?

Deer are both grazers and folivores. They eat grass, flowers, and leaves. In winter, when they cannot find grass or leaves, they eat tree bark. Butterflies are nectarivores.

Bees are palynivores. They eat pollen during their whole lives. They also eat nectar.

Glossary

Note: Some boldfaced words are defined where they appear in the book.

carnivore A living thing that eats animals

digest To break down food in the stomach and intestines so it can be used

endangered animals Animals that are few in number and are in danger of disappearing from Earth forever

energy The strength to use one's body; the power needed to move and grow

food chain A pattern of eating and being eaten

grains The seeds of plants such as wheat

grazer An animal that eats grass in a field

herd A large group of animals that feeds, travels, and lives together

intestines The body part that takes food from the stomach and through which waste is removed from the body

mammal An animal with hair or fur, which has a backbone, breathes air, and drinks its mother's milk as a baby

nutrients Important parts of foods that keep living things alive and healthy

savanna A grassy plain with a few trees that is found in hot, dry places

Index

Printed in the U.S.A.